AF487260

We ARe nOT PeRfEcT,

but

THE UNIVERSE IS!!

VAISHNAVI R

Acknowledgement

I heartily express my gratitude to my family and friends, especially my mom, who is always supportive; the one who gave me her wings to have myself a high view and to soar high in the sky. Thank you, mom! I will always make you feel proud. A very special gratitude to my school Principal, Tr. G John Prabhakar, the one who encouraged me a lot in my school times and let me see myself through, while the reflections are still transforming me into a new form one after the other expansion of thoughts in my mind. And I thank an incredibly special friend of mine, who never gave up on me and really helped me a lot to confront all the difficult moments while drafting this book. This is my very first book and so, I would like to dedicate this book wholeheartedly to every reader of this book.

Preface

There can be many significant colors with different, extensive shades in lives of dissimilar people in the entire world, whereas everyone expects their realms to be only in a particular color that generates seeds of ignorance in the minds of those people. Here, I wish to share about a state of ignorance, lacking an enlightening perception as its presence gives us the supreme knowledge to respect others' choices of colors and shades in their lives though we could not even put confidence in presence of those shades in them. But to respect others' choices, each one should know that he/she is not perfect, also he/she is not supposed to be perfect in life to just breathe and live life to the fullest. So, when we find that we are not very perfect to the eyes of each other, we do have to accept that we are not perfect even to ourselves. But there is something being latent and continually active in our life that the universe is so perfect that we will get anything in reality very precisely in order to our **thoughts, actions, and responses** of our forms. So, I wrote this book, expressing my perspectives on the topic of "We ARe nOT pErFecT, but the universe is!!" — that thoughts can actually be seeded in your minds; breaking moments that can truly make you into a whole new form; a source of creation that is all about you and only your potentials; happenings in the wild and dark woods and the wild flowers that can really make you strong and finally, an attitude of being a leader and also a laborer to your own realm!

I hope this book with my personal perceptions about all transformations in and out of buried seeds as a metaphor for the thoughts that can be buried in our minds that could transform every one's life, would guide you to have a mastery perception on every favorable and also an unfavorable happening in your life.

Contents

Chapter 1

Buried sunflower seeds never bring roses at their tips! - the thoughts.

Chapter 2

Dare to be broken for million times! – the darkness.

Chapter 3

You – the only source of creation! – the light.

Chapter 4

The Dark woods and the Wild flowers! - the holy pain.

Chapter 5

Be the leader and the labor of your own realm! – the consistency.

Chapter 1

Buried sunflower seeds never bring roses at their tips!!

Life is to live, and living is all about embracing every moment in life. Not surprisingly, embracing every moment in life is not quite that simple for us and the only reason for us to not have the idyllic moments constantly in life is simply that we are humans, the living creatures with a prodigious faculty rather than any other creatures to dream high and to own burning desires one after another to reach out to them eventually but, only by overcoming a lot of challenges in midst of the journey, to get a better and the best of all the dreams formed in reality. Starting from a form of thoughts about a dream in every mind to own it in a real world in the end, none of us can lead that journey serenely. We will have to conquer all the difficulties not only in this materialistic world but also within each one of us to get a better form of goals in reality. So apparently, we are not perfect to ourselves in every present universe with our known abilities to deserve our own dreams to form its real state in reality **flawlessly,** only unless we are perfectly ready to be the souls to accepting and embracing all pains and failures as a perfect growth we need and owning the pains within ourselves during a journey to get reached out to our own bright destinations---Growths don't mean just an extension in quantity rather it is all about an expansion in quality from within and also an expansion of one's life in 'reality' if the one wills to explore within and also out of the mind and soul – the body in materialistic world. When you dream about a life in which nothing will make you experience anything other than an idea to run towards death instead of experiencing and embracing every moment in life, then the life is nothing but a golden free ticket for a feel good movie in which you just shut-eye for the whole movie time.

In this life, a golden life, to get yourself expanded with quality, you should allow yourself to see through your pains during expansion: It is always YOU and it should be 'YOU', not just because none could describe your pain but only you can feel anything precisely that is within you — Just like nature, seeds see through themselves in the dark to sprout out shoots towards sky and roots below the Earth which will get itself expanded to its extreme capability both above and below by all means of a path called, 'Sustaining pains with grace and will'. As then, a buried seed turns into a well grown tree and will be blossomed in land beautifully. Here is a relation between growth and pain, when you grow, you expand, and when you get yourself expanded, you 'change', which is certainly needed for you to live serenely in your every future form and 'change' is the one that can put you in reality of your dream but those changes need some sacred battles to be fought by you — against you, within you, in which you could be wounded or bled with pain in your every present form. When you dream about your goal, you certainly expect 'change', and when you fight for the change, you must go through pains in you, just because 'we are not perfect with every present form but wishing, rather having a burning desire to become perfect in every future form'. Moreover, when you dream about growth and expect the 'change', but not willing to fight for the change, will plainly make you feel unalive in your present form. That simple!

Dare to fight against all your odds; heal yourself with aids of morals after the sacred battle between you and you, rather than being downhearted in your present form

where you are actually stuck between present body with a mind willing only to dwell in an expected future but, not for the changes needed: eventually, there is 'no you' anymore!! Be you, dare to be you and own only you just with all your dreams.

Whenever we dream about a better future, universe always paves many considerable ways to everything we dream about, that to be formed in reality, also only if we are willing to love pains during growths. Pains are not thrown at you for a sake of fate or any kind of similar concepts, but it is a positive response towards the change, that you are moving towards your destiny because when you don't feel any pain and be very ease at your comfort zone, it certainly means you are not stepping up for yourself. When you do not hold yourself up to perceive a lot from life, I would like to remember you once again that you are no longer embracing your golden ticket in this heavenly life. We do not have any other choice in life but to expand, grow, move on however and whatever; why not choose a way to enlighten ourselves with a faculty of embracing every moment including pains during the lifetime or why not choose a way to at least try for it??

From a far and above perception, we are definitely too perfect with our past forms and dream prodigiously about a better future to be perfect in our future forms. We may not be in perfection due to our flood of thoughts, but the universe is so perfect that it always owns everything, even beyond perfection and allows us to perceive a lot from life which would eventually make us perfect just to deserve our dreams grandly.

The one and only proof for the universe in perfection is that the universe never says "no" for your hard work, disciplines, integrity, and love, which all four in your life will certainly put you in what you majorly deserve!!

Anything can be seen and felt must be sourced out from somewhere and also be gotten strength by something for its long life, just like a buried seed sources out its shoots and after then reaches its ability to grow and forever strengthens them with its roots for making them to be blossomed. Similarly, your transformation of dreams into reality wholly depends on its source, your thoughts – buried and retained in you to eventually make yourself reach heights and good depths for better future.

Here, the blossoms can be seen only if the seed gets itself disappeared (according to the outer world) and deliberately concealed (according to the inner self or world) in dark to let out shoots and form a base, the roots by the art of transformation. When you bury and retain a thought in your mind, you start to transform yourself to become as like as your future form according to your source thoughts. Because the universe is always wide open in every single way and you are gratefully blessed with a faculty to have a burning desire to move on into that wide open space just to feel and live serenely in reality, in accordance with your very thoughtful desire. All you must do is to just enlighten the faculty to move on into that wide open universe! An end of anything depends only on a start of something on its own: the sunflowers in heights can never be shot out from a buried seed of roses.

Like roots of plants, let your inner self be the source of power and provide strength for your enormous growth in the outer space, the reality just like shoots of plants. Furthermore, it has to be noticed that only the shoots and roots undergo an act of transformation, not the physical realm! Like seeds, we can not be born in accordance with own willingness in physical realm, but we can change it gradually though with a strong will to make ourselves sturdy and fruitful in the end. So, when you have an organized thought or a great idea about something, it is not the physical realm transforms but you do transform in decree of your source thoughts. When I mention 'source thoughts', it's not about a thought that you had a long time ago and not anymore, it is actually a thought that you own in your mind for every moment during a journey to reach your dream destination. When a fully grown tree or plant is very fruitful, the universe somehow will definitely change its surroundings for better; same as that, your physical world too will be changed for better only if your seeded thought turns into fruitful actions. The act between a seed into a shoot with a root is **the art of transformation**, which means, 'Changes'. The changes in your actions accordingly, will lead yourself to your own destination in future.

In most of cases, shoots of plants are seen but never their roots, meanwhile roots are the ones that hold its shoots from Zephyr to gust with unforeseen love — beauty of selfless love! In that case, let your inner self be the source of power that strengthens yourself out in reality.

Own all the colors of feelings in you, for your soul becoming darker with pains of many paints, the more your body glows up on this land but only when you let light through you!

We all know that we could not program our minds to perform its flood of thoughts. But we should also know that our thoughts can be concerned, also cannot be concerned by us for good and better results in future. Every thought is a seed that could be buried in your mind and can be concerned to become either a life-giving flower or a poisonous flower in the future. A buried seed could become a great and good tree one grant day only if it is concerned for its nature of shooting out life-giving flowers. In contrast to that, if a seed is retained and concerned well in spite of its nature of shooting out poisonous blooms and shoots, it will not give the same results like the good one. It's not only important and not easy to select only good thoughts amongst flood of thoughts in mind, rather we could be careful in what we perceive from all the thoughts we consider and be concerned with only the good ones. Additionally, in excess of results of our dreams in reality, our thoughts can turn into a big and original form in reality only if it is concerned accordingly or properly for its progresses. For those growths to be progressed, the concerning part can be done in both ways — one could be 'by you and only you' and the other one could be by anyone who tries to sculpt your form with his/her own mind's form: just like a tree grown on its own in the wild woods and a tree grown under a preferred concerns of an other being. It is amusing that both the ways could become good or the best or even the worst. Apparently, it is better to regret for not doing it better on yourself rather, to regret for not doing anything about it. Remember that there is always a chance to choose a good way when there is a hope for a good result and there will be always a better result in the end. A good way could be also chosen by someone who did many things against integrity in his past; who then really tries to pull himself together by perceiving a lot from all his flaws and iniquities of his past but does endurance to reach out his dreams in reality; someone who grows up with integrity in his mind and kindness in his heart even after facing a lot of problems — one of the greatest act in the world!

You are good when you find your mistakes; you are better when you try to understand what made you do that, but you are the best when you accept it eventually to give yourself a rebirth and willing to love this golden life once again!

Thoughts that we engender from our mind and thoughts that we reckon from materialistic world must be formed and acknowledged respectively, only if they the thoughts are along with righteousness and integrity. Integrity in life is a quality that can not be sourced out in physical realm, but only from a self, owning a spirit to live life truly that really means living life fully — Inner self without a quality of integrity lives only a speck of life as only an inner self with spirit of integrity can grow and glow everywhere in space.

"Walk with integrity or walk behind a man of integrity; All the other ways will lead you to be in deep water."

The power of thoughts you seed in your mind will reflect in the fragrance and blooms of flowers in your own destiny. In materialistic world, your mind is a slave as well as a ruler and these bearings of your mind, a slave and a ruler can be decided only by your own mind's choice and that is also hidden with a secret for peaceful life. In your mind, whatever the images or voices get absorbed from and reacted to the minds of physical realm and the times in repetition of those visuals and actions, will eventually create and reflect the best attributes of the expected form in your body and mind certainly but an ideal attributes could be attained only from within.

When your mind is absorbed with images and voices that is formed intrinsically with virtues, it will definitely get you to the peaks of many peaceful mountains and also when your mind is absorbed with images and voices that is created intrinsically with iniquity, it also will definitely get you to some peaks but of macabre mountains. And those peaks of peaceful mountains can be perceived only when your mind's form is like a slave to repetitive wishes that is, recapitulated by you; and, apparently the peaks of macabre mountains will be reached out when your mind's form is like a ruler in its own flows with materialistic attributes. Here, if you are well known for whom and when your mind should be slave or a ruler, you will perceive a mastery perception. Instead of being as a slave or a ruler in accordance with reflections of this outer materialistic world, be the both for yourself as after then the game changes: when you become the both bearing within you, you will be the great leader to lead yourself and the loyal laborer to strengthen yourself. Furthermore, if you are not acknowledgeable about for whom the bearing of your mind belongs, you are neither living nor surviving but certainly being just as a machine in someone's world.

In contrast to the mind in materialistic world, the mind is neither a slave nor a ruler in the pure spiritual world. It is because when your mind bears a form as a slave or as a ruler, it appears as a form in an other state of your soul. The mind is you and you are the mind and that is the secret of peaceful life in spiritual realm where being grateful for everything is all that matters.

In a world full of guides and their words for forming our minds to be at their best at any of our goals, have you ever thought about reason for our concern towards our thoughts in mind and efforts that we put really very hard to make our minds very 'controlled' ones while which is also led by other people minds' words whose minds are never controlled by themselves most of the times??

Instead of listening to the words of others and putting every typical actions under the limits of their words, listen to yourself, your thoughts and your universe as you will be knowing 'you' in the process and eventually lived your life to the fullest as there would be only you when you look back! Don't make your mind to rule you or to be as a slave for you under influences of others rather, you be the leader and the laborer for your own realm. If life is not meant to live it to the fullest, then what else it would be, even though there is death for us all in the end anyways!?

"Thoughts are the seeds that has to be concerned genuinely which then apparently put you into actions to

be in reality like shoots of a plant in the light of the world, only if the process is fed with power of your feelings."

And those feelings could be either good or bad; however, the results will be the reflections of the power of the feel. A good feeling includes being happy, warm, pleasant, peaceful and what not. A bad feeling includes being sad, aloof, unpleasant, chaotic and what not. Apparently, we cannot easily let go of our negative thoughts yet we have the ability to acknowledge them as what they are, which will pave us the way to be blossomed again. The entire world is heaven when you are in a good feeling but the whole universe is hell when you are in a bad feeling, why? Because good feeling makes you forget everything and only the bad ones make you remember everything which fortunately includes every bad moment in your pasts. The one and only best possible solution for facing the bad feeling is in the way how you approach it. Try approaching it in a unique way and keep trying it until you understand how many heights the bad feeling can make you reach out more than a thousand good moments. So, feel the bad moments as it is, fall for it, cry out a loud, make yourself a solitude space, but never settle yourself there. A seed will be inside a mysterious dark world for some time (not always) to make itself expand to give itself a fruitful life eventually and to others too. Prove it, not to your people, not to your pasts, not even to the universe but prove it to yourself that you always deserve to grow and glow more. At your last few days, the size of dreams does not matter, what matters is how you feel before, through and after perceiving your own realm in reality.

To achieve any of my goals, I had a notion that good feel would eventually result in a beautiful destination only and the bad feel to an unpleasant destination only, out of the blue. But when I looked closer, I recognized that destination couldn't be reached out without a traveling journey that has many unpredictable ups and downs, turning moments, even verges of life sometimes. All the bad feelings happen to be noticed as failures, hurdles, stumbling blocks but really they are the ones that will make yourself enhance and enlighten in the exact needed parts of yours to not just own victory at your destination; further, it will make yourself feel that **you deserve it** by showing its strength in reality. Every bad feeling will turn into the perfect puzzle that needed to make yourself complete and strong enough to face anything in upcoming future. Apparently, your strengths depend on your power of feelings and the best way of approaching it in a different perception. So, I believed that the spots when you feel bad is the moments that you start traveling towards your own destination, it certainly does not happen out of the blue. There is always a choice for you to change your destination amid your journey just like at the stations for trains to be stopped. The bad happenings could happen only if they are fed with the power of feelings heartily or repetitively until it is reached out by only you. Your goals can be achieved successfully with power of feelings fed by you heartily and the bad thoughts amidst 'you and your destination' can also be grown vigorously if they are too fed with the power of feelings, no matter it is good or bad!

After all, every life in the world love to be lived with their own good feelings, it's better to appreciate and respect other's feelings and adore your own feelings. The buried sunflower seeds do sprout out shoots as the rose seeds do; grow greenly as the rose plants do and so shoot out those flowering buds as the rose plant do but the sunflowers will not be as like as the roses in anyways at anytime and vice versa. The sunflower is the Queen that falls in love, follows direction of the Sun, a king! And the rose is a crown that makes king's queen feel loved by the king! Where there is a Queen, there is love and where there is love, there is a King and a Kingdom too. When comparison takes part in them, there would be a presence of scale to measure their nature which then results in a concept that everything is same but just with different levels of quality and quantity, but for themselves, it is actually not!

The thoughts that you embed in your mind will be reflected and precisely in the reality and any difference in the reality takes place only if the feelings are not fed zealously. We could not be ideal in visualizing the goals in what we need or want but the universe has the supreme ideality for our visuals that paves way for the chances to be taken at right times to take part in our lives for us to reach out the goals more precisely what we asked for only. Morally, sunflower seeds deserve to fall in love by direction of the Sun and rose seeds deserve to make Queen fall in love with her King! They deserve their own nature and form adorably. If there should be a comparison or a judgement to be taken part, let it be done by the outer world but not definitely within you, just like those sunflowers and roses.

Somehow, it is believed ignorantly that there would be no good feel presence after a terrible moment like failures that just happened due to many reasons. When you try to be in a good feel after a terrible moment, it doesn't mean that you need to laugh a lot without any reason, it does mean that you must either accept your mistakes and your flaws whole-heartedly and move on without any regrets in case of no similar chances in the future or try to avoid the mistakes in the forthcoming chances and form yourself to the best of your expectations. Either way, it is a win-win! That means either of above-mentioned ways will definitely take you to next better state of yourself. But, you might be the rich or the need; the loved or the lone; the seen or the selfless; the pilot or the plane; the sea or the sight; the sky or the speck to yourself, there is a feel that has to be recognized by you as a human being and that is, 'you are blessed to share breaths while your companions do live on the same land during good possible time with you and you also could express what you feel here on the Earth, the land that spaces for and bears the feelings of infinite divine souls'. Why to worry about next level of freedom in physical realm while your prior freedom is already there for you to just **love** yourself which is same as loving the entire world??

There are numerous alluring views on the Earth to be seen and felt and also some souls to be loved who don't get the ideal births like normal beings do, even not knowing themselves and struggling to survive until their last breaths, conversely it is amusing that we ourselves get stuck with a speck of illusionary visions of materialistic happiness and satisfactions which is the only one that makes us feel terrible — a speck of problems as a universe full of thorns and spines but in fact those problems are the signs that the universe wants us to learn and grow out of our comfort zones just to reach the peaks of mountains one after the other to know ourselves better. When we at least have a chance to know ourselves while some people struggle to do it, why don't we dare to take a chance to know ourselves and those who struggle too??

We do concentrate on the guidances of others, in fact, many different ideas are pointed out for making our minds to go through an infinite narrow way which is never going to make us feel the real happiness though we could reach out our destinations one after an other. Some people are fully focused on the mentioned points that would just lead them to their goals rather than falling in love with the process of growing which will only make them feel to be deserved for their goals. The destiny could tell others what your aim is, but only the process can tell you who really you are!!

"Don't push yourself hardly to the feel, just feel it!"

We appreciate and celebrate all the good feelings in us and conversely, we do either run or try to push away all the bad feelings. Apparently, the only reason is that we love to be in the feel of Love and we hate to be in the feel of Hate. And from a different view, some of us hate things that some of us love it to the core.

So, along with appreciating your good feelings, be glad to appreciate and embrace someone's good feelings even if it's a bad feel to you just because you do not like it. It is not suggested that you should support the wrong paths, but you have all the ways to respect someone by which anyone could be respected with every piece of their own piece of souls. Respecting someone does not only mean to greet them or just to show respect only when they are around, it does have a high state in which you start respecting others' wishes whereas that is one of the aspects of love. If you are a sunflower and expecting your friend, rose to follow direction of Sun, it will not happen as your friend rose deserves to express someone's feelings and even if that happens for your happiness, it doesn't mean rose fall in love to grow towards Sun against its true self, it means rose fall in love with you and priors you to its own self!!

In addition to it, if you do not own a different perception, you would not be able to perform this embracing mindful exertion. Here, it is just a distinct perspective not a mastery one, we don't need to be mastered for understanding our loved ones when there is **love.** But when you are fully formed for owning this different perception, nothing in the world can maneuver you in your views and ideas. Instead of being at the core of good and bad in an either way, try to balance it and rule your tranquility in your own way.

In a nutshell, 'buried sunflower seeds never bring roses at its tips' doesn't mean the sunflowers are good or bad in comparison with roses and vice versa. Yet, the nature's way of expression about thoughts in this quoting is simply that the thoughts we own in our mind, forms its own figure in reality beyond the competition between good and bad opinions. Additionally, not only a buried, retained seeds shoot out towards light and hold itself extraordinarily strong in darkness, even a thrown seed own **will** to grow giantly and could be also difficult to uproot it off!

Some of us love the energetic and elegant faces of sunflowers and some of us love the elite colors of roses, but in the end: good or better does not matter, rather the feelings are! If you do not wish to explore yourself, you can not find what you are, which will then cease you to live your life to the fullest.

"Choose your thoughts – beyond rights and wrongs, also choose yourself with integrity."

Chapter 2

Dare to be broken for million times!!

Whenever you are breaking down into pieces, that you don't feel yourself all together with all your thoughts of past, in present and for future, remember that the universe is helping you to make yourself so strong that you will just deserve your dreams in the end. An ordinary stone can not bring out a stunning statue unless it gets itself hit by a sculptor for more than million times; a diamond can never attract the eyes of people unless it perceives more pressure by the nature; a plane can never fly in the sky unless it is ready to fly against the air in the high sky; a buried seed can never grow in and out unless it has a 'will' to shoot out itself and be in blossom!

It is apparently hard to undergo a process of 'healing' but certainly there is always a choice to go through the process, in which 'mind and body' is to be aligned ideally that would inherently bring peace and happiness in our lives.

"...let the weak say, I'm strong."

- **Joel 3:10**

"...my strength is made perfect in WEAKNESS."

- **II Cor 12:9**

Let the world break you again and again, be strong enough to resurrect from each of your fallen pieces; fear not ,for this battle: you had already fought the battle in your mother's womb – you won the battle and blessed to be here, just by getting yourself broken into many cells. While your birth is already a success, and death makes you feel terrible, why really do you fear for dwelling a life before death?

A seed in the other side of the land could be raw, lonely, held stiff in darkness, having no growth or development for a long period of time but if it owns a will power to be alive to shoot out itself, the raw state would become a fully grownup tree, the lonely state would reveal a power of solitude, the state of being held in darkness would become a hidden base strength, and the state of no-growth will unclothe it's own power eventually.

"Never lose hope in darkness at any cost, for the times after you are losing the hopes is the real darkness you would ever confront: Not the ones at your present illusions – the fear."

Sporadically, life throws you into the dark, just to pave way for you to understand that the lights outside over there may burn you into ashes, with all your dreams! We are not ideal with our thoughts and decisions, but the universe is, always! Not only to save 'you' but also your 'dreams in you', which can be built with the base of your 'thoughts' only.

Consider yourself have gone into a wide and large sized space where thorns and spines are filled in and fully occupied with darkness, where you probably have similar feel to it whenever you are pulled into negative thoughts and opinions like failure, anxiety, pain, self-reproach, regrets and so on..;when these feelings stand at all the magical doors and hide you from the lights of knowledge, pull yourself together and sprout up as a shoot not just from the dark but also 'through the dark' from within and should become a profound enduring statue in the lands blessed with source of light, even your branches and leaves are dead and gone!

From every frame of mind, life is a combination of both hurdles and happiness, but from a mastery perception, 'hurdles are in the dark sides which make yourself deserving your happiness in the bright sides'. They both are not as like as the just two sides of coin rather, it is the love of roots in the dark for its flowers to be bloomed in the light while the strength is believed in the hopes within the soul — it is all one single thing!

One of my friends had a supportive and prosperous family and friends. She got very elite surroundings for her stepping up periods of life, so that there could be no predicaments on her way; yet also she is struggling to fill herself with her own bearings as she is so much obsessed with her colleagues' aims and dreams. Most of the people confront the same complications in their life journey in a way of stop climbing up to their own peaks separately, and obsessed with climbing up to the peaks of mountains of others. In which, they are still failing even though they reached out the peaks of other's mountains ahead of the real seekers. All of such kind of people efforts and hard work may be sometimes more than the real seekers, but it's all the other's aims and dreams however, where is yours, where is you, where is your burning desire, where is your journey after all..?

"Climb up again and again until you reach out your highest peak in you, but never even try to imagine climbing up to the peaks of others' mountains which would lead you nowhere!"

We all do run behind a common wish of every soul that is to eventually dwell in a golden palace in each one's own way and everybody on our journey forgets to pick up the 'pearls' that is left on the shores after every little storms in life: recognize them and embrace the progress which can only make you acknowledgeable about the growth and power of your own crown – made strengthen up of the 'pearls'.

When there is life, there will be pains and when there is pain, there should be love and when there is love, then all the pains will become gains in your life at the end. Love your pains and live with them instead of running away from it - just let your pains guide you for becoming the ideal minded soul that is truly building you, for deserving your expected goals.

It is not every time your mistakes or culpability for being broken rather, it is the lesson that life is trying to teach you to move out of your comfort zone whenever your mind tries to attract the expected dreams. Also, life will try to push you away from your comfort zone in a way that there would be a drastic destruction of your present universe which would hit you very hardly; concurrently, there will be a formation of your future universe on the exact reflection of your feelings that is recognized and expressed during the pasts and the part in between the destruction of present and formulation of future universe. This is the moment when you really need to believe in your dreams and yourself; also, stand firm against all the negative thoughts and opinions and do not let your present self get itself fall apart together just because of your present universe falls apart. This is the moment with a gift of great opportunity to throw away all your bad stuffs into the destruction. The present state destruction doesn't mean you fall apart all together, there is always a tiny bit of 'you' — the ideal you, who knows every happenings of your life and just willing to live a better life in the upcoming future states: adore the ideal you from every destruction for making a better future forms, just like a shoot of a plant changes itself to be a sturdy branch eventually.

This is also the moment when you feel like yourself falling apart and no way to be even alive but in real and in contrast, that's the best moment which should be recognized by you for happening of the formation of your new healthy and also prosperous life. This is the state of nowhere but towards somewhere which is highly appreciable and worthwhile; the state that reflects your strengths and weaknesses to yourself; the state when your soul get pushed to a stumbling block with no intimate feel on your own body, where you probably feel yourself belong nowhere but that would be the aforesaid better state when you will pull yourself together to make yourself rise above the stumbling block! You win or you win, no matter what!

Holding on in a circumstance for a prolonged period of time would become familiarized and practiced to you unless it reaches a state of comfort zone. Every comfort zone is sourced out from the intolerable levels of hardships and elevates its goodness eventually after pains and hustling challenging work but again it ends with a bed of roses, called a comfort zone again. In basic observation, the overall performances of one's amelioration in life can be recognized by his or her cycle of comfort zone which could be considered from either a typical lifestyle or not basically a run-of-the-mill lifestyle.

A typical lifestyle that is fulfilled with supply of all of the basic needs of a human being or even a predicamental lifestyle with no proper financial support, and no satisfied job can both be ameliorated only when the person is ready to move out of his or her comfort zone or experiencing the part of illusion called fear. Let us consider the first stage of comfort zone is ordinarily a typical lifestyle that has composed with supply of basic needs of people where everyone would feel their own kind of lifestyle is just like a bed of roses.

The next stage starts when the person is brought down due to predicaments on the ways to achieve the one's expected better prosperous destination in the nearing future. This is the stage when crisis occur to make the man stronger than his previous version by battling against his present lifestyle to perceive the expected destination, or at least to hold on his basic needs.

"When all things fall apart together, it is actually creating a larger space for the best forms to be progressed for future universe, only if you do believe in its actions."

The third stage starts when he becomes familiarized in managing the plight and tight corners of his current new lifestyle, which then ends with a state of being on a bed of roses again! The next cycle of comfort zone starts in the near future just after you wish to get or attract something new which is not already there at your present state of life. For every cycle of comfort zone, there is a progression and amelioration in the form of expanding the supreme knowledge and its consistency. The more the expansion of knowledge and the power of amelioration, the higher the peaceful life for this birth! The cycles of comfort zone are one of the happenings in the nature that occurs in everyone's life either consciously or inadvertently.

However the situation you get stuck in, whatever the difficult situation it is, whenever the time it has to be confronted, if you are ready to form a better life out of your comfort zone; if you believe in your forms and manifest it, then you will be in your future universe no matter what!

"When you wish for blossomed flowers in you with all your hearts of integrity, be armed to seed yourself, for you have to fight against all odds including darkness on the other side of the real world-within you!"

The pains get vanished when there is love, the love on yourself and the love get disappeared behind the clouds of happenings with pains. You have to be dared enough to be broken for million times during those excruciating moments to reach out the peak of your mountains. For every goal to be achieved successfully and heartily, it has to be paid by hard work, dedication, discipline and 'the will' in you to do all the foresaid attributes. Remember a phrase, 'try and fall apart as many influential pieces rather than being left with a whole heart brimmed with regrets.

Heal your pain with love – Love Yourself, that reflects you in loving the vast universe of nature, which in returns will never stop supporting you and your flows. I heard many people saying, "But, how is it possible?": yeah, there is a map which is inscribed in everyone's mind intrinsically but never recognized for its presence, the map which will lead you towards an answer for their questions; that is, in life, at any situation or any unbearable afflictions, there is always a choice right within you, even at every single moment of 'decision making' – a preference for good habits rather than bad habits; a preference for being in love with everything, even with pains rather than loathing your pains; a preference for willingness to do something rather than sitting behind with reasons and so on.. Those good preferences looks like appearing in the sky while you are pulled down to be in deep waters by the bad ones, but the fact is that you can be wherever in the world with your creativity and imaginations to fly high in the sky, you must remember that the distance between the good and the bad preferences is not like the illusion like between sky and deep ocean, rather it is within you — the only matter is that to be aware of the distance illusion and bring change from within. You are not thrown into an ocean of pains, left behind with no hope and supposed to be jumped up for reaching the sky, you are actually in a state of knowing you and your power of being you! Bring a change and have a balance in life.

"Don't be overwhelmed for what you do not have at the moment; whatever it is, you are just one step away from your goal, a step of ACTION! Throw a stage for your actions to be performed, a stage of BELIEF! Receive love and peace for your actions on beliefs, a state of UNIVERSE IDEALISM."

An idea of perfectionism that includes feelings here on the Earth, can only be felt by each soul, can never be created by anyone for others: We, the humans are inherently pulled to either bring all the broken parts, for trying to unite them just exactly like the way it was, the olden whole one or be broken more than the remaining broken parts and loosing ourselves as it never makes a whole single thing again: but we are never encouraged for the acceptance of being broken which would definitely reflect the distinctive dimensions to be felt and to be acknowledged about the boundless energy of the Universe.

The idea of perfectionism in an individual's thoughts is not supposed to bring unambiguous states of progress while the thoughts are being manifested in one's life. In reality, the concept of perfectionism is the possibilities of all the ambiguities happening in one's life just to make the person fit 'perfectly' to the state of his own higher expectations, through which the one will become synchronized with the expected results in the reality and then he or she will be perfectly worthy for their own upshot in every future form.

Yes!! The efforts for the journey towards the destination of perfection would be very hard, also it will certainly try to break you into more pieces at every stumbling block before reaching it, but these are the best moments that would carve you to fit into the ideal forms as per your mind's commands through your thoughts manifestation.

In addition to that, life is not only about chasing the next high peak of mountains one another, it is all about making yourself strong, accepting your flaws, learning from mistakes, accepting your regrets, feeling great pleasure in healing your pains and in yourself, growing yourself, sculpting yourself and also *'loving yourself'*, which must be the best faculty in you that can make sure all the aforesaid progresses happen peacefully and benevolently.

If life tests you on your compassion for your future universe or form by pushing you into an ocean of problems, even you were broken after all your hopes had been gone, just try once again after all the failures, for the test is not concerned with results like success or hope, rather with your compassion for your future form: instead of longing to be on the shore for dwelling like others do, fondly pick up all of your fallen pieces and train yourself as the best swimmer who makes a lot of adventures in the ocean in which you were thrown into. Yes, it feels difficult to change the tough circumstances according to you to perceive your future form, but there is a chance to do it. As it is difficult, it does not mean it is impossible. The chance must be '*a change*' in your view — not in a optimistic way, yet in a mastery way. If everything is planned already and everything can be defined word for word, what would give us adventurous experiences beyond those perfections both within you and the reality??

Simply, if everything happens very accordingly as your plans, it is certainly a success, but if anything comes along in midst of the process, it does not mean that it would earn a failure, it could also be an adventurous success eventually. So, instead of drowning in all your flaws, failures, regrets, mistakes and stumbling blocks, just swim, swim for a very adventurous success in the end. If you loose your hopes after a lot of trails, just do remember to live happily in the deepest sides of the ocean too that you are alive with a will to grow and expand and that's why it's hurting, when there is growth, there will be a mass progression leading you towards your goal with all your broken parts being worthy for your upshot; because, an act of drowning will definitely kill you but a feeling for willing to grow will certainly bring a successful adventure before death. The aforesaid willing to grow doesn't happen just with an extra confidence or hopes at all, rather a dare to be broken a million times, for filling up all the new parts of you in the midst of broken pieces, as there will be a better expansion of you — your future form: pick up all the new parts of you that you gained some of new 'you' while facing hardships and stumbling blocks during the process of perceiving your future form and fill them up between your broken pieces to get yourself expanded to growth.

In this world, some paths have to be passed through lonely with no voices of materialistic world but only on guidances of your own voice which is the only one part in the journey that defines you to yourself. The path of solitude is not a spell rather, a bliss to change your present form to make a better and the best future forms later. A seed in darkened space do sprout out even under a lot of shadows just to live its life towards light and make its own dancing shades in the end! You are going to raise like a shoot and penetrate like a root and do fell apart from within in the end like any tree but there is an infinite life to be lived to the fullest within this journey and you better do it anyways!

When you stand alone, you need to confront the predicaments in your way on own, yet you will be deserved for your goals wholly. After manifesting your thoughts, you will be into the reality of your dreams in the nearing future for sure, along with that when you manifest your thoughts and endure pains all alone more than anyone during the progressing period, you will be at the state of providing chances for those who just wished for their dreams to come real. When you cannot find a way to go through or live through, dare to walk alone, and make a way for other to live a life like you do.

"When you just wish, you will be one in a swarm of bees, also when you wish and own endurance as a unique faculty, you will be the queen bee to be followed by the swarm."

Do not blame for being alone rather, appreciate it that you are with solitude. That is the mastery perception, own it!

Make mistakes; in a great depth of healing fact, accept all your mistakes. Explore the previous plans and actions within you to find the places with faults which might be the reasons for your plans to be ended with unexpected responses from your universe. Mistakes or failures are not reactions for your actions towards your goal rather mistakes are the supreme guides that will direct you effectively and support you to perform the best actions during the journey and failures are the finest comrades who light your paths, the right routes, also lurk the wrong routes in a way of shining the right routes that could be seen by you eventually and follow the reasons for failures which will lead you directly to the desired goals. Some happenings come along in your way which may not actually have a definite fine reason for its causes in your life but remember that you do not have to define everything in your life, sometimes something does not deserve to be even defined!

Never sit idle after committing mistakes or facing failures, you are not moving forward only when you are sitting idle, and you are moving ahead though you are actually in the same state but you do accept those mistakes and failures in a view of the supreme guides and the finest comrades respectively.

"If stars are aligned perfectly instead of being scattered, there will be no eyes get shined in the reflections of twinkling stars, after a certain period of time!"

Dare to be unique and put the world always under wonder at your dazzling realms. Furthermore, being different in a throng apparently attracts all other's supporting and opposing opinions to be fallen into your form: but embrace those wounds as of only valuable depreciations which really would hold a point to make you stronger. Also, agree to receive the words and opinions to be as chisels, and you – dare to be a mindful sculptor who certainly neither loathe the hitting chisel nor worry for the pieces that falls from your effigy, but fully focuses on exonerating the falling pieces that are ready to let go of the soul for good and be objective of being mindful and peaceful whatsoever.

Let your broken parts be broken, but never stop endeavoring for your goals to be achieved by owning your broken self with present best attributes in a way of giving life to every single piece of you and later, watch the success growing amid of all your fallen pieces that would make you eventually into a whole new piece in a giant look and also a strong form again and again.

"So, make yourself tighter during gales; make yourself freer during a gentle breeze of wind. This attitude will form you to weather the storm instead of standing idle during a heavy downpour!"

If there would be a presence of perfect love, especially as light as petals for your heavy pains, the search will definitely end at your inner deep self, for you are the most well-known form to yourself. When you recognize it and start embracing the self love, it is the state when your soul is going to head towards a divine power through virtuous faculties of mind and the body. I'm not trying to frame your mind to not to have credence on other's love in reality but I'm guiding you to embrace self love so that you will be not expecting the whole perfect love for you from others in the world and so, it generates selfless love in returns which is more needed in the present realm we dwell in. Do not dare to be broken for something that could make you live with no love after certain period.

Some people get disappeared beyond dark sky like stars at an act of Illuminating revelation of true love. While performing this act, you do simultaneously throw yourself beyond sky as a burning star, but while the person you love concerns 'the moon'! This is great until now. But when you wish to shine out only for the person, even not for yourself for a whole lifetime, you could see yourself vanishing somewhere in the universe: To love someone, there must be 'you' first of all, only then it means you love the one. Be strong in the act, for when you give up yourself once, you can see yourself getting lost into the space for ever. Dare to love yourself even at the worst dark period of time because when there is love shining out of you, your enemies could be found of their true colors and your loved ones could be found as of your colorful rainbows in life forever. It is as simple as a seed falling in love with light while falling in love with itself as deep as its roots!

The best form of love in reality is to love the other souls with all its scars and wounds in the past as their wild flowers — you can do love the other soul wholly only when you know your ideal love, the self-love!

"When love is all about understanding the other soul and doing the perfect need, then I'm damn sure to tell

you that loving yourself is the perfect love you would ever receive in reality!"

When a never broken and the best sculpture is being appreciated by people in the lands behind the materialistic world, a million times broken but still a **willing soul** will always be appreciated by cosmic energies in the space, beyond the world. So, be proud to be accepted as a broken piece of form, also pull yourself together to get broken for 'million times' in the journey to divine destiny rather than being given up on yourself even just for once.

Giving up lies totally on the other side of the wall for being broken: being broken means that you are endeavoring to reach out your destination and feeling listless, for the pains and wounds happen in the midst of your mindful journey whereas you are not really broken or dead but giving up reflects that you are truly and undoubtedly broken in the mind's realm and being idle with broken parts but still you can be recovered on your form only if you are willing to do it with all your pieces of soul together.

All you want to go through is the transition path where you accept all your scars and embrace the marks as wild flowers which eventually will gain you with all the strengths to always fly like an eagle and soar above the happenings like a heavy downpour in the material realm.

You may fall apart and break into pieces for a lot of reasons including, being raw, lonely, held stiff in darkness, having no growth for a long time and so on and life may tear you apart with all of its reasonable and some unexplainable happenings, but dare enough to be blossomed in light rather than pulling yourself down with nothing but an illusion of fear for something which is actually not anything. Struggling to own a much dare like that? Well, there is a reason for it: that is, you no longer need to dare for your wish as there is something beyond it, waiting for your sights and endeavors — you just deserve more than what you expect now! Dare a lot until you brim up with adventures, telling you, "Enough is not enough"!

"Never fear for falling apart, and when you fall apart, make sure that your form with strength also falls apart and grow vigorously for a million times in your fallen parts!"

Chapter 3

YOU – the only source of creation!

When you have a goal to achieve, you will live through a stage of 'transition' that simply changes all your actions and responses everything around you, but candidly the source of change is only 'YOU'. If you change, that primarily changes every piece of your soul, you will own the knowledge that gets ameliorate for every moment when your form gets itself expanded. To bring that change in you, it may be very tough due to many reasons, but time plays a significant role in every situation of life just by pushing you to change as there would be no chance for the changes later. When a seed is buried in a dark side of the world, it never just come out to get the light, rather it changes its own form into something which is supposed to be in the light and also, the seed never just show up but also it holds itself very strongly in the dark from within too.

No one in the world is worthy enough to give you the freedom to choose 'change' within you. But time owns its power to give you the fear to choose 'change'. Even though you find obstacles around you that stop you to change, the voices that lock you up into a cage of reality, the images that engender from your own mind that expose all the negative chances to fall into, remember that you own the power to endure all the aforesaid predicaments and sprout up from the dark to shine out in the light.

"You will change only when you will to change and if you don't change then too, it's all your culpability."

You will reach your destination only when you know what your destination is! Or else the life you get would be filmed eventually with just wandering remembrances which reflects a life with no means of the gifted body for your soul. We all know that the goal you aim in your mind must be fully and precisely visualized within you and then put actions in reality, about where you will perceive your goal precisely; in an other frame of mind, you don't achieve your goal rather you create it in your reality. In a null shell, you can create anything in your reality whatever you want manifestly in your mind's eye. Additionally, always prefer creation to existing destination if you like to own uniqueness in your mind. The visuals in mind can be formed in reality, though you own only breaths in your body, not any chances to be even close to the destination — all you need is just a 'will' to play your role on your stage of belief.

"If life is an ocean, some get ships, some get boats, some get Catamarans, some get ships, boats, catamarans all together and lose everything like a bolt out from the clear sky, also some get nothing then own everything to the heights of sky: so, remember that with-nothing is always better than becoming nothing. Both can be confronted if there is an attitude of willingness!"

A decision to change yourself could not be raised up from a mind full of regrets and pains rather, it should be from a mind which is obviously in an ideal form to accept mistakes and endure pains. Sometimes, we expect past situations to be differently happened as we could never accept the way it makes us feel whenever we get thoughts about it. Though we do not have any option to change the past, we fail to perceive an idea that now we all own our present moments to be embraced for the future universe, then the present again becomes the past later. Along with it, never forget that you are entitled to owning many elite standards of attributes at any time even after crossing any activity of iniquity which could be even widely known to you. No one is perfect for all the time; no one's life too: some get to confront unexplainable bad happenings in life though they were so true in past that they do not supposed to be confronted pains. As it is said earlier in the second chapter, you are always welcome to choose good faculties at any time by your life only if you are ready to do it from bottom of the heart. The universe never says "no" for a good thought and ideas anytime.

"Your past is an irreplaceable and permanent inscriptions in your life; every present and future part in your life will certainly become your past; so heal your pains of past by falling in love with your present, eventually it will form you in a better way that it will make unique and admirable inscriptions in your later past!"

Is not amusing for you that a bird just walks all the time during its excursion though it has vast beautiful wings to fly!? It is similar to the situation of yours when you have wings to fly but you are afraid of falling down and not flying at all; you can have a change in view only if you fly from present land to your future flights! Sometimes, it is not the bird forget about its wings, the own wings are never recognized by the bird just like how you are not aware of your faculties.

Like I previously mentioned in the last chapter, throw a stage of 'BELIEF' for your actions to take part. One among negative feelings in everyone is fear: fear to be buried under, fear to be in darkness, fear to be sprouted up, fear to be even shine out in the light sometimes! But in fact, fear is just an illusion that your mind exhibits a film of all the vexatious chances to fall into your brilliant progresses whereas it is apparently indeed that you bear the real power to face all the fears which is in illusionary state. The real power to confront fear is to believe in every single piece of you and only you. Above and beyond the power to confront your fears, you should own strength to withhold yourself for dwelling out in reality, the strength that gets stronger by only endurance of pains within you. Also, once you recognize your power within you, you would never be affected by any terrible illusions rather you will be appreciated for your dazzling creations. It is either illusions or creations, it is referred as it is only because of the feelings it gives us back for our imaginations all together.

Let the present universe get you all the abundances in your life, but you can feel it only if you are in a fit state to perceive it. Some may dwell with a lot of abundances in their present form, but they would never recognize and concern what they have with them. This may not look like a big deal in life but conversely it is a big deal in life because if you don't know what you have, you can not create what you want or need and even if you get all your needs and wants in future, you will still be idled after then as you are with a lack of self-awareness. This state of yourself will lead you to live less than survival in life.

Dare to deserve your goals in reality. Though you get some things in life that you feel you do not deserve them, dare to deserve them all with all your hearts of love and integrity. Consistency gets stronger only when you really deserve your goal. Recognizing what you have and perceiving what you aim for are the great actions you could ever do while you lead towards your destiny.

"Actions are the logic but also a magic bridge between a mind's realm and your destination in reality".

Any dream can be achieved successfully only when it is in a state to expand its form to **physical existence** in the real world. For a peak to be reached out, we must climb up the mountain though it pulls us down with a lot of obstacles, out of which some of them are tethered to our legs. For that, we should untether all those pulling strings of obstacles with help of the great attributes such as 'forbearance for predicaments' and 'perseverance with goal'. Untether yourself from pulling strings of obstacles and at some time, you can not untether yourself from other kind of predicaments – Let those pulling strings put you in the right directions just like for a kite to go high and fly, once you deserve your power, soar high in the sky and this time let those pulling strings know that you are a free soul to perceive your goals but not a kite to be always controlled by someone. We all know this following quote: "You could run towards your goal, if you can't, then start walking towards your goal, if you can't walk though, then start crawling towards your goal but never stop or walk backwards" because if you can see it, you can go forwards and get it. It is that easy in one way!

"If you can see it and couldn't get it, you are either with fear or without fortitude!".

There are many possibilities to get stuck in between your mind's realm and reality, the prior to every possibility is, you with no-growth. Growth is nothing but an expansion in you and when you expand, you create an extra part in the old you to get yourself changed. A creation of new you amid old you can be happened only by you when you dare to be broken and let lights of supreme knowledge to reflect you the right paths to be followed for growth and expansion. During a progression in you, not only the best steps keep you move forward, but also your flaws can move you far more than the best steps, when you have a mastery perception in your musings of your flaws.

Many of us must have felt sometimes like wandering in a realm full of nothing but chaos, it is the stage where we apparently don't know where to move and how to move in life. In that case, it does not mean that you do not really know the real you: like not knowing what you want, what you like, what is your wishes and dreams to be achieved and so on.. that even includes what you deserve. Truly, it is just a moment where you have a choice to choose between a lot of things. You will know the real you when you go through those choices one after an other in your life. Just recognizing a thing as it is, is better than getting lost into nothingness for ever!

Life is to live and love, not to win and survive. But, if you are still happy even after not knowing what you want to chase in this materialistic world, it is definitely a particularly good way of living, until it harms someone else's life. While happiness can be found anywhere in the universe, why do we need to search for it out as it is also there in you, a lively speck in the universe??

Defining yourself is as same as counting numbers in math until you can. A human who is seeking for 'something beyond everything & nothing' can not be defined or even described word for word. Never wish to fit yourself in a container, you are here to be free and own your freedom like you own everything in and around you. You cannot define everything about you, but you will be written continuously with a comma forever.

Instead of showing hatred at predicaments in your way, have forbearance under those predicaments to follow your plans, because no power in the materialistic world can bring the change either for you or around you. Reasons for the changes in you could also be in the out but the changes can be happened only in you.

You own all the power to create anything and everything in the material realm, and along with that you also own a supreme power to recreate anything you shut down within you.

"To find what you deserve, live through the paths of endurance rather than standing still in midst of the journey towards a destination: sometimes you perceive the changes in you while you go through the journey just as you deserve something far beyond the destiny!"

Never ever doubt your abilities, instead put confidence in your willingness to do anything in the world. You might be blessed with any physical flaw but it is with you to make you feel yourself, also fear not to spread your wings as you are blessed to have more strengths than others to soar in the high sky and fly above the impossible physical world. If you have a dream as everyone does but when you are passing along with any flaws in body, you are blessed to own more strengths to withstand the hardships that come along your ways, by that way: you are more stronger than others and remember that the flaws are allowed to be only to the level of body but not to the soul in your body. So, trust your 'will' rather than your wings: your 'will' will make your dreams come true in reality as the universe like a sky is so perfect that it is always welcoming you to take high flights in life and never shut you down for your flaws in body. For your feathers being with you as like as a will, then what makes you to be in the ground by just looking at the sky? While the universe never says no for your endeavors to fly high in life, there is no odds in your way that has a strength to cut your feathers!

"Don't try to ignore your flaws, instead dare to become strong enough from within to persevere with your goal along with your flaws, as this attitude can take you to a real high flights in sky."

As every goal from a petty wish to a burning desire is in need to be created, organized and maintained by ideas only in mind, why should we even consider about flaws in blessed body!? The body is just a tool to do things after your born ideas. If you have an idea to be its best form, there are many ways to make it happen: it's just in a need of an extra efforts to be put in your ideas to form it in reality; though you make it happen, you will be in a state where you are you, with a strength that can never ever be destructed by any power in the world.

The thoughts and ideas you bear in your mind are needed to be prepared wholly for its figure to be in the reality. Those ideas have to be constructed really in this physical realm by many attributes such as willingness, strengths, compassion, burning desire and so on... but if that construction doesn't hold trust or belief on its progression and results, it means that it is welcoming all the possibilities to make itself fall apart.

For an instance, if you do not have trust on you and your ideas with progression, basically you will not focus on your target, instead you will be pivoting around all the possibilities of negative happenings as a matter of course. Then all those happenings will take in charge of every piece of your soul to ruin your dream on your own. Trust is neither rooted for concealing precautions nor a false feeling in your way, rather it is a good feeling that can make you still move on even after a lot of discomforts in life because moving on and living is what life is for, not to be idled just for a prodigious goals within a one time golden ticket choice of life.

And now, if you trust on you even against many negative chaos wandering in your mind, you will make miracles that will prove that 'anything with trust' can be done successfully in the end. Also, I'm not telling you to believe everything you see, everything you hear, and everything you even feel sometimes in life because there is nothing can be created newly in personal life as it can be only felt deeply to the core of you but I'm certainly telling you to wake up your idea with power of trust to see the miracles of Nature's happening in this physical realm of your professional world.

If at all you can not trust your new ideas or thoughts or goals that can be sourced out only from you and being afraid of facing its consequences, read yourself again clearly that you are not strong enough to believe in yourself and your strengths and power too. Belief is a stage for any of your ideas to be performed in front of this world audience, so build your own stage and put confidence in your act and let the remaining part of appreciations be in the hearts and hands of people in the world. Fearing for upcoming results sometimes could lead you to be idled where you are. Dare to fly even if you do not know you either do own wings or not! Because, when you dare to do something, you expand your strengths to withhold yourself during those high flights, among which daring and willingness as potentialities to fly from a ground which would be readied to confront anything that could come across its ways.

"An inferior idea dressed up with a thin cloth of trust can play a vital role in life in comparison with a better idea disguised to be in a cloth of trust."

In my past, the was a girl who lived in a city and had an elite lifestyle from birth. At her twenty's, she was so free that she could take her decisions for her own life. Also, there was an other girl from a family where there is a financial struggling, who had a typical lifestyle from birth, similar to aforesaid situation, she was also owning her freedom. They both desired for the same goal but really from a quite different ways to reach out the peak of a mountain. Both suffered but the latter one suffered a lot comparing the former one to reach the peak, yet they both reached it successfully and wished each other for their successes.

But what if they knew each other and stay connected now and then!? the happenings would be hugely different with occurrence of competitions in their lives. At every moment, they would be comparing each other's abilities to climb up the mountain: from spectators' point of view, the competition would just reduce the time period for them reaching out the destiny but from selves' point of view, they both are competing with each other just using their abilities in a way of passing a perfect time period which actually will not give a space to know themselves from within during the holy battle that leads to success however the end ends.

During both instances, apart from competition, if the two girls try to know each one self, the journey will take them to a great heights even more than the successes they own and above the peak of the mountain to soar in the sky though there is a heavy downpour in the ways of their destiny.

"Do compete: do compete with your struggles, do compete with your self destruction, do compete with yourself because it's the only way of competition that offers you more time to know you rather than a competition with another soul."

The prominent creation which you could do among all the forms in the universe is that you can carve your form 'again and again', also at 'anytime' and 'however you were' just before the chance to change or carve yourself. The substantial potent in you is that you can even carve your form to make people to recognize and remember some paths that lead to the supreme knowledge of the universe.

When I mentioned that you could carve your form again and again, I meant that that you could really recreate anything you had formed already in you. The reasons you think for not making it — may be that you could not go through the process 'again from the outset' and 'nothing.' But the real is you can offset that feeling in you by remembering that an idea is just created within you, only the formation is made out in the real world. So, no one could stop you recreating any of your ideas from within — no one can neither recreate nor destroy your ideas until you have a spirit of love in and around you.

"Create, confront, recreate but never get convinced and settled down just with all your trails."

As I mentioned secondly that you could carve yourself at any time, I truly meant that that you can do what you have to do with no limits in time periods of your life. All those time limitations in day-to-day life are formed only by us from a materialistic point of view in the world. Due to an urge or to overcome a predicament in life, we have to follow those time limitations in materialistic world. But simultaneously, we stop the growth of seeded ideas or goals in our minds which would eventually become perished before we concern them back again. If life is not to live with passion in you, what else can make sense at last few days of your birth?

Imagine yourself owning a golden award for swimming though you are just an expert of doing it with a lots of practice but from within, you just really love to do painting on a canvas. Even if you hold the award for swimming, you can not feel the sublime happiness and satisfactions that really need to be felt deeply to the core. Also, even if you don't hold the award for painting, you will really be on a cloud nine and you will feel the sublime happiness and satisfactions like getting an award for every single time whenever you just have a look at your colorful work on the canvas at your home. The feel from within as a passion – fuels your dream to burn brightly which would eventually become a golden crown for you on one fine day.

"If you are burning from within to reach out your destination, pour the fuel of passion for owning a dazzling realm later in reality"

Finally, when I mentioned thirdly that you could carve yourself however you were, even just before the chance to change. I meant that that you can reform yourself however you want you to, though you were at any kind of extreme possibility in negative thoughts, opinions, and happenings.

You may had dealt with the worst days or months or years or decades or even the whole life you had got, or you may had the worst character beyond the pale just before recognizing the chance to change yourself. You can still reform yourself only if you need to do it for yourself by moving on. Yes, you can make your worst reminiscent go far away from your mind only if you do walk away from it: Walking away from it, doesn't only mean that you need to pass your precious time as just like that in a flow, it means that you need to live in your present for each and every moment you breath on this land.

Additionally, I mentioned already that we all have a choice to choose the better ones at every single moment. So, recognize that and embrace your past life and move on as you have an exceptionally long way to go, and you do dare to believe in it. Just by living in the past in your mind, not having culpability on your life in reality, you are in the pasts full of fallen leaves in search of fruits while life actually brings you many blooms and more fragrances in every present Universe – all you want to do is to embrace the present universe for a fruitful future universe later on. Season changes and lives too!

"Though you don't have a beautiful life, be grateful for your blessed birth on this land in the cosmic infinity of universe, just to feel!"

While a buried seed's growth is apparently well seen on the land with a appearance of sprout, there is a wild power grows in the other side of land with flows of root wishing to grow towards the core of world. Just like that, to see light out in the reality, you do not only grow towards light but on the other side, you grow wildly from within to expand yourself towards the core of supreme knowledge. For anything to be sprouted out in the light of nature, it must be buried within anyways, either within land or within you: but both the acts are same when it comes to power, the wild power from within. Furthermore, for a shoot to be sprouted out, to perceive the power of light and to be blossomed lately, the buried seed's root has to be grown within first. In the same fashion of shoots and roots of a seed, for your dreams to be in reality, you must act from within first, as an act of power. To own the act of power, it is not as easy as anything to be done in light, rather it is as tough as anything to be done in darkness and there is a choice here too, just to ignore the darkness and explore the wilderness from within, like how the power of roots not just sprouts out and also holds its shoots very well into the light of the world!!

Do not search for or run back or try to hold on a miracle while you are the real miracle! You can form anything even the best future universe, only if you believe that you can do it. We are free to dwell in imaginations and creative happenings in mind which then can transform into its real form in physical realm.

CHAPTER 4

The Dark wood and the Wild flowers!

The power you possess for sprouting up above the darkness of ignorance, for you to be kissed by the light of supreme knowledge is the one which will just make you see the light eventually; whereas, transforming and growing towards the light is very significant part of all together. Later the part of sprouting up, you will be tried to be pushed away, pulled down, buried under, plucked off and what not! But once you recognize your strength and power, you can never be rooted up for anything that could happen in the outer world. You could be stormed by gust which may try to uproot you from your present form, but the gust always reveals your strength to yourself and to the world just by how you hold yourself up there in reality and deep within you too. The gust could blow through you as people, places, or timing but all you want to do is just to hold yourself up from within with all your brawns like a tree does hold itself up with a power of its roots from within.

Then, there comes a moment when you start knowing your own strengths by simultaneously possessing and expanding it in every piece of your form. It is the feel that makes you to be on the cloud nine for every time you obtain a progressive growth after some changes and happenings in your present universe. You can fly only if you are ready to face the air that blows towards your flight.

"If you are walking, with wind that blows along with you is your luck; but, if you are still walking, with wind that blows towards you is your strength."

In a journey towards your light and elegant destination, with all your actions that keep you moving forward, you would get interrupted by many things like the present places that hold you tightly to not to move; the present people from whom you can't just walk away; the present situation from which you can not get a clear view of your destiny. Along with those struggles around you like aforesaid situations, there are also an other dark side of hardships that will hold you back to not to climb for your victory — that is, within you. Any predicament that comes along your way has to be either from the outer world or from within, you.

Whenever you have a dream in your mind's eye and being so brave to perform perseverance to create a better form of your dream in reality, you will be facing a lot of problems that may only be arisen either from out of nowhere around you or within you. These are the only choices that may try to devastate the progresses of your dream construction. Every time you get hit by a stumbling block, try to figure out the source like how and where it comes from: either from reality or from within. Along with that, be dare enough to fight against it and gain more strength to be in a better form so that you get hit for another time but you will be holding yourself stiff for this time instead of getting broken like in the last hits. If you are facing a hurdle in reality, it does not just mean the hurdle is only in reality. You feel that as a hurdle as you do feel so. But there is no such thing in your reality sometimes, rather it is the thing that you have to do it to get it done. It is that easy. An actual hurdle in reality needs only your strength to show yourself and to the eyes in the world for holding yourself up at that difficult time; but the hurdle you just feel from within you needs only your power to bring to light you and only you for expanding your form from the previous time.

"Show your strength to the eyes in your reality; own your power from the eye within you!"

During those bad happenings in life, the only attitude that can put you in a state of freedom is 'daring, daring to live life to the fullest in spite of a chance to survive or die'. Dare to face up again but with an expansion of your strength, like how a buried seed sees light again by sprouting up its shoots and by rooting in the other side with a dare of owning power to withhold itself. Some of the plights which are sourced out from outer world in materialism should be left behind on ground if you wish to take a flight high above everything with every piece of your soul – that then drives you to sour high in sky.

Every new thought or an idea buried deep in you that is wished to be blossomed lately will put you in a state to go through a lot transformations within you, only you and without you, in reality. Pulling yourself together through all those transformations lead you to be yourself as a great person to deserve all the upcoming good, better and the best happenings in life eventually.

Those buried thoughts all together as seeds grow more in you just to expand itself as a wild wood where there will be some wild flowers and some dark sides too, which I name as the dark woods. You are not just about a single thought of you, you are a wild wood where a lots and lots of thoughts had been buried and will be buried too, can be seen only by you, some grown, some not grown, some are so wildly within deep in you that you can't even see on your own.

Like how in reality, seasons change and bring out changes in lands of nature, the wild wood, which is you, do undergo season change which you may not expect it or to change it according to your wish. Due to which, we get pains, wounds and scars that remain in our souls until it heals ideally. The season change in the wild wood reflect yourself the perfectly imperfect moments or happenings that will make you certainly a perfect fit for your goals. The only two best choices during your season change journey to make yourself a perfect fit of what you dream of — is the art of 'ignorance' and the art of 'acceptance': ignorance of all the actions that is always pointed towards you just to distract you from your progress in growth, acceptance of all your pains, wounds and scars as your wild flowers. Additionally, be sure in not responding for those actions which will not help you to step up in your life, rather respond to your flaws and flows for stepping up in your life in a way that you will be in an ideal state eventually, in where, you will be too high for those actions to be even considered.

Seasons do come and bring changes in you, no matter what! All that matters is that you feel as beaut as petals during spring, as hot as gold during summer, as tight as a diamond during winter and as light as a feather during a fall!!

To pursue the deep concept of all about broken moments in one's past life, there must be some wounds and scars as wild flowers bloomed at the one's heart but they had been always kept out of sights, that is... They are covered behind incoherent flows of thoughts with a fear for materialistic world. Those wild flowers are needed to be loved and always concerned for their presence within oneself. All the predicaments that you face in your past life are blooms within you that includes your pains, wounds, and scars. Those wild flowers are the pains, the wounds, the marks of your mistakes or bad happenings that bloom every time within you whenever you are stuck during those tough times. The reason I call them wild flowers is that your pains and scars are meant to be concerned and accepted in all conscience as they are. The wild flowers in you are longing for your concern so that you feel you and do move on with courage of being you with every single wild flower of you owning a power to grow more and more. No matter how long you try to get rid of your wild flowers, you can not grow more than your present form unless you concern them, adore them and be dare to own them as yours. In fact, when you don't dare to concern and adore them but try to get rid of them, they will be withered some other day which will make yourself a unlively wild wood eventually. Because real growth happens only when you leave behind your regrets at the very moment of recognizing them and hold those wild flowers to make yourself a flower wreath as a crown to grow more, just like how every shoot hold their flowers as it's crown at its own tips. In a different perception, your wild flowers are not actually pains but a colorful change that happen within you which own a power to make you grow more and expand just like any other wild flowers do!

"A thought as a seed can grow into a tree with flower in its shoot and power in its root and the flowers of the shoots can grow the supreme and wild wood of you, only if they are concerned and adored by yourself as they should be!"

Many of us can understand what all is exactly about our wild flowers but we are not ready to go near to them. The reasons may be fear, the fear of the feelings that those wild flowers gave us in the past, the scents of them that make us go back to the past and bring a flood of remembrances which stops us moving forward, the scar of their presence that makes a mark in the present piece of soul in the present universe. But I came a long way and when I turn back, all my wild flowers are appearing now as beautiful and magical buoyant steps that I had followed to reach my wildly grown present universe while my bad ones in the past universe was getting simultaneously destructed itself. So, when you have wild flowers in you, just feel their presence, embrace the enduring paths that has been shown to you and also be grateful for the very past wild flowers as buoyant steps that has brought you to the universe where you are now.

Give your mindful recognition to your wild flowers and embrace their wilderness within you, which then reflects in strengths that grows from your mind in soul's realm to the skin in body's material realm.

Don't try to have a long step by trying to get rid of any of your wild flowers as it will be a hard process to be stepped on the aimed one definitely, also if you miss your aim, you will be fallen down into anywhere in the darkest sides of your illusionary universe from which you could be stuck having a chaos that certainly hides the light for the supreme knowledge within you. It would be the moment where you should fight against yourself to come back to your mindful form later. You would be the exact source for sprout ups of your wild flowers, so you owe them anyhow; or else sometimes, they will make you to recognize their presence and fragrances that would pull you back to drown in the flood of past remembrances which apparently will stop you focusing on your present version. Be dared to deserve them as your beautiful wild flowers that give you unapparent wings to fly to your future universe every time you need to.

After having an idea to be concerned in your mind, you may sprout up to bring to light the idea into reality after a lot of broken moments within yourself to hold up against darkness within you, to shine out in the light and then you will not be just as strong as a big tree all of a sudden, you will have to perform growths in all the possible ways to build your strengths up to withstand all kind of predicaments, both from outer and inner realms that may come along your way. As it is mentioned earlier in this chapter, that you are the wild wood with some wild flowers and dark sides too. The dark sides are nothing but everything on the other sides of 'you' in reality, the shoots: that is, you from within, the roots. Those dark sides where your roots in dark and lonely from within grow more to hold your shoots up in reality are named as the dark wood. The dark wood is simply that it is you from within, in darkness and lonely for all the times of life. **"While the first and foremost freedom is to think what you do think, why do we always try to get rid of the deep darkness and silent solitude within us?"**

Against both ways of predicaments flowing through you like a gust, the growing periods in you establish the holy battle within the wild wood, you to reach out a state of supreme freedom in reality and life.

To sprout up against all the dreary darkness including the ignorance of supreme knowledge, you have to go through holy battles within you — against no one but yourself! I call it as holy battles because none gets hurt in the battle rather, you will be raising up from nothing and grow beyond everything like a seed into a big blooming tree and do repeat. Before or in the midst of the holy battles, you may have a flood of negative thoughts as the bad seeds in you which may grow more and more if they are concerned with all your heart. Furthermore, with a good perception in your mind, you will come to know the good ones and the bad ones that apparently leads you to have a meaningful life everyday.

During those holy battles in which you try to live your existence a little more and more as of growth and expansion of your form, you may win or loose. As we do know, you will win if you are in the battlefield with your heart full of will power and you will loose if you are in the field with mind full of negative thoughts. If you win, you gain nothing but an expansion of your form of existence in reality and from within too and if you lose, you lose nothing but nothing at all, not even the supreme expansion of your form of existence from within, however. It is because when you win, you do celebrate and move on; but, if you loose, you do have a chance to change yourself to try again to win. That changing yourself part is the best adventure that you can ever try within you!

If you do not will or dare for holy battles within you, you are actually being still like roots that do not grow more, rather than expanding itself from within. Then, your every part for what those holy battles happened, will be shrink into nothing but a scar eventually. As it is foresaid before, this is a holy battle as none gets hurt, none win or lose, but you do celebrate your triumph eventually only if you own a mastery perception of life. Because an expansion of your form into a space in the universe needs just an act with a spirit that tries to live life meaningfully, however. **Life is not to win or survive but to live and love!**

You will loose beyond everything and nothing, not in the battle but only if you are out of the holy battles. When you are hit by a stumbling block by your way, either in the outer world or in the inner realm, you should have a dare to put yourself into the holy battles where you will live or survive to live life to the fullest eventually. If you do not dare to put yourself into the holy battles, you are neither living nor surviving but will be fallen into a state of nothingness.

This holy battles will be happening within you, within your mind's realm in which you will be put into battle ground to leave behind all the negative thoughts off the ground and put confidence in yourself to raise above them which will make you fly in sky — from where your negative thoughts will be found as small as a speck to the eyes of you, soaring in the heaven. Only then, you will realize that you do deserve high flights and some heights later too.

The power of negative thoughts could lead to ANYTHING as it is just an illusion. Out of nowhere, you will be forced to watch a film of all the possible negative happenings that could come along your way of success to cease you performing a perfect progress within you which could make you reach out to your destination. There is also a high view that the more your confidence and possibilities, the more the negative thoughts would be, but also have double dare enough to live through it!

When you give up on yourself and drown in an ocean of negative thoughts, you will be fallen into a frame called illusion, from which no one could save you AS IT IS JUST AN ILLUSION. The negative thoughts are the illusions in your mind either due to fear or lack of somethings which you think that it might fall into you from your reality.

Simultaneously, you will be giving out a big space for the happenings of all those filmed negative thoughts in the outer real world to perform their actions truly in your reality which will be pulling you down eventually. The only person who could save and protect you then from falling into the ocean of negative thoughts is only you! The moment you recognize that all the negative thoughts are just the illusions, your frame of mind on your confidence will just go to the belief stage to rock your performance — the actions!

While heading towards a goal or destination, a good thought falls into a frame of dreaming and a bad one falls into a frame of illusion, and it has to be in that way because of the power of good and bad feelings from both the thoughts. Good thoughts make you stronger to move on towards your goals and the bad ones pull you back into nothingness. So, better prefer good ones to bad ones as power of feelings is stronger than we could ever imagine.

Leaving behind your confidence and holding yourself on with those negative thoughts, you are actually doing nothing in reality as you are fallen into the ocean of negative thoughts, the illusions. This act of yours only causes a lot of predicaments as you naturally move on towards it and make them fall into your place as reality stops for none no matter what! With a good perception, you can recognize the negative thoughts as illusions; then, you will throw a stage of belief to perform your act willfully and reach out your triumphs one after an other holy battle!

"Have a good perception in life to live life to the fullest, rather than having an illusion to neither live nor even survive but to just fall into and get lost in the same illusion forever!"

Your hardships and mistakes are the imperfect carvings in your story, yet you should really get many hits with pains to carve yourself just to become the best perfect form of you. If you are struggling with hardships, it will be truly a very hard moment for you to cross the ocean, also if you just even did strive to reach out the shore eventually, then it will be really a very proud moment for you for crossing the exact ocean. It always seems impossible in the beginning, easy and less acts in the end.

"With remembrance of your hardships as carvings in your story, carve yourself out of a better form in real while crossing the ocean!"

However the holy battles might be, if you are found by yourself from within more than the previous state of the dark wood for every holy battle, then you get to put yourself all together with new pieces of your form getting ready for the real battle of consistency. You can fly only if the air flows towards you, so fear not for the air and embrace the gentle breeze between the heights of your altitudes.

Chapter 5

Be the leader and the laborer of your own realm!

After sprouting up shoots from a buried state, though the plant reaches its own level of potentiality to grow as a tree, it just does not become a dead wood all of a sudden. It still lives on by daring to encounter changes within it due to happenings of every season's change in reality; it lives on and do encounter changes until it has its will to be alive within its living potentiality. Similarly, we all do undergo a flow of changes during growth periods of our journeys even after holding our triumphs in our hands at destinations. Though the journey heads you towards a destiny as a victory, the real victory lies on — being in it whatever happens and deserving it until you can.

For a plant to encounter changes in reality, it does not only need strength in its shoots to withhold itself. It also needs power within its roots to make itself happen in reality. To pursue the concept of strength and power of a plant deeply, the plant could become a dead wood even it loses either one of them in its shoot or root: which is exactly, its strength and power. So, for a person to confront anything that could come along his way, he needs strength in his form in reality as much as power within him.

"Own your strength like a loyal laborer and own your power like a legend leader to be as legit as a lord for your own realm."

Your form, which can be made and expanded within you, can never be fallen apart, for the destruction that tries to exist in reality. It means that nothing in your reality can destruct your power and strength to grow more from within and hold yourself up in reality respectively. All those destructions may happen in your life in reality due to a lot of possible terrible happenings and it may also bring you down with nothing left to do. Even after that, you can still reconstruct your dreams in reality only if you are daring to discern your form from within with all your strength and power together. A plant cannot be considered dead if it is not sprouting up or not blooming out due to many possible reasons; because it will sprout up one day with a spirit to be blossomed again like anything more than other plants do. You can never be destructed by outer world unless you die: for you to be lively in this life, it is all your choice to dare enough to live it to the fullest till you reach your living potentiality. If you live on and on like the plant with a spirit, you create your own universe behind you; also, when every step of yours is energized with discernment both from only within you and every single thing without you in the world, you create a universe to the greatest degree which then will be remembered manifestly in every mind of the world to be recognized and to be followed by lots of people towards the divine source of peace and happiness.

So, either the construction or the destruction of your form, both can happen only from within, by you. Dare to encounter terrible happenings in reality to be lively in a path that throws lights of knowledge in the darkness of ignorance which directs us to head towards the supreme knowledge by crossing the ocean with every piece of you owning perseverance and persistence to reach out the shore that holds your realm tremendously.

In the journey of crossing an ocean full of problems, the better support that your present universe offers you is the air that flows to the sail of your boat which paves the way for you to move forward, but the better choice to own belief is all yours, to heartily sail the boat; if there is no support from your present universe, then the better oar you could hold during the sail is like to have fortitude to withhold trust in you, yet the better choice to own willingness is all yours; furthermore, the better states in you could be the passion, the imagination and the creation as teak shafts to be put together with strengths and endurances as your latent potentials for building up your boat anytime, while any one of the shafts or the potentials missing could lead yourself to drown in the ocean. Morally, the shipwreck that can be happened either due to outer world obstacles or even only by you eventually.

"Falling into an ocean is not a failure but willing to settle down in deep water is!"

It is all about patience and consistency to feel the successes to the core. After sowing a thought in your mind, concerning it and waiting for its flowers to give you the fragrance of happiness and freedom, you need to bear the long period of time that the universe offers you to make you live with abundances in the end. In the middle of the progress, you may be distracted by million possibilities to perish your growths and peril your strengths. So, the better possible way to withhold your form against all those distractions and to avoid aberrations is the acts of patience and consistency together with a mastery perception of a clear foresight in your mind about your dreams.

"For every pilot, it is not about only flying high in the sky as it's all about landing safely to the destiny."

Having constant thoughts, ideas, plans and notions on your goal is certainly necessary in you but apparently, only those can not form you to achieve your goal. You should undergo the process of transformation in which you would change the form of ideas into physical realm and that is the moment when you must withhold persistence in you. Those constant thoughts and ideas are like seeds buried in your mind and never watered with concerns for their acts unless you put them under the process of transformation by actions in reality. Their sprouts that shoot up in your reality must be looked after by you to achieve its supreme growth as a tree along with your latent potentials like strengths and endurances which can be owned by you with a great attitude of consistency.

Mistakes and regrets are the wild flowers of you, as they are the flowers that bloom only within you. As only you can feel their presence and fragrances, you are supposed to concern them with an embracing perspective, with poise and grace, for their presence and blooms paves the way for growing yourself as an extensive wild wood to live life to the fullest. Never try to get rid of your wild flowers or to move away from them or to ignore their presence: if you do so, you will never grow or expand your form, for only they own the potentiality for you to bear fruitful future universe only if they are concerned during their presence. Additionally, the potentiality of your wild flowers can offer you new seeds from its fruits to not only just expand you but also to have yourself an other possible ways to achieve your goals: we are not perfect with our wild flowers, 'mistakes and regrets' but the universe is always perfect as it never shuts our way for growth, rather it always has us to own the possibilities to reach out our goals eventually. So, adore your wild flowers as your crown like how every shoot own their flowers as their crowns at their tips. Acknowledging your mistakes and regrets is the first act to support their blooms in you and embracing them with a growth perspective is the second act to own fruitful results in the future universe.

"The more you adore your wild flowers, the more you expand your form. The more you expand your form, the more you expand yourself to the core of the supreme knowledge."

Never give up and settle down only because of your mistakes and regrets. By believing in yourself, you can perform consistent actions towards your goal, yet that consistency can be withheld by your foresight wise of the goal. While struggling in living through the dark woods of consistency to reach the light of nature, you will be offered with many wild flowers, which are mostly ignored by many of us but in fact, they present us the great treasures of attributes such as strengths, endurances, love on wounds, healing power and so on.. Only if you do approach and accept them as all yours, they bloom as beautiful as beyond anything in the world.

"No more steps in the upcoming path doesn't mean that there is no way, it actually means that you do own

wings now to take flights and to reach some heights in your future universe."

Whenever you are about to deal with major changes in your present universe, remember that your future universe is building up its state and expecting you to dwell in there very soon. So, deal with the changes with poise and be grateful for whatever it offers you, even some wounds and pains, as they are the ones who give you the power as like as a leader. So that you will be in a state to balance yourself between the destruction of your past universe and construction of your future universe.

As every time the universe offers us the choices to choose any one of rights or wrongs, it offers the same thing during the state of every change that happens in the present universe but the major moment full of choices that plays an integral role in the time period of forming our future realms. So, whenever you are thrown into a state of dealing with your changes, you need to be so wide and above board in receiving all the chances, yet try to move only forward with power as like as a leader and have strength as like as a labor to withhold yourself against anything!

Fear not for the changes yet fear only for the stillness that could take control of you and make yourself feel like lost in nothingness to be an empty soul, without even a recognition of your own form. All the changes are not to be just confronted but some of them are to be accepted as it is, some of them are to be tolerated for just some time, some of them are to be embraced from within, some of them are to be fought against it, some of them are to be just loved, some of them are to be recognized for something new, some of them are to be proved for your strengths and every one of them are to be known to make yourself feel YOU.

"If there is a change, even by breaking you, it is going to bring light in your darkness through broken spaces and fix yourself with new glasses of your reflections for making your form more substantial and colorful."

One of the best aspects of growth in your form is that it apparently explores the secret of going forward; it directs you to move only forward and never think about any other sides of possibilities which could perish your growths. Once you reach the goal in reality, your growth still does not stop over there because, after then, you will have to grow more from within by acknowledging a lot in life to have a consistency in your goal. The efforts for the consistency only can make your goal alive or else, you would be facing the destruction of your goal in reality gradually.

You can grow only when you are ready for changes in life. The decisions you take during those turning points must be incredibly significant so that the form you get in the end would be really grown with power to withhold any other bad happenings which may lead to the destruction of your form later. Apart from taking decisions to lead a progressive growth in life, you must put yourself into action. If you do not perform acts on your stage of belief, there is no one going to know you, including you too. There is nothing going to motivate you to put you into action except you and your will to live life to the fullest. Either you put yourself into action or no one and live your life less than survival.

Though you had many changes in your way and not yet grown even a little more, your next change might be the one which could give you the whole new universe as you expected earlier and all those changes in your past might be the little forms that to be put together to feel your whole new presence in your future universe.

"It will definitely take time to glow if it's about to glow everywhere and forever!"

Being responsible for both of your actions and the responses, which you get from the universe for your actions lifts you to the state of consistent growth in your life. For an instance, if you are not responsible for your actions, your actions will not be in a certain way rather it would go with a flow or it may go in a way that eventually ends at nowhere, and if you are not responsible for the responses that you get from the Universe for your actions, then you are not going to grow, also you will go weary in trying hard for your successes. You can never grow until you are being responsible for everything you cause in your present universe as qualities of growth includes being responsible for all the happenings in life that can head you towards being yourself stronger than your prior states.

When you are responsible, you will be filled with high qualities such as punctuality, concentration, persistency for every part of work and eventually you will be with a crown — the discipline. The practices to attain discipline involves responsibility in every activity you do, that will teach you to control the unnecessary thoughts which are wandering around in your mind. Taking control of your thoughts is must, as apparently the thoughts without control can cause you to dwell in chaos which will not allow you to focus on what you want. Responsibility is not only for failures but also for successes. Yet, there is a perspective in acquiring a responsibility in a certain way during a particular moment — be responsible as like as a laborer for all of your successes and as like as a leader for all of your failures.

"When you have the best challenger for your chaos in your mind as your discipline, you will never ever be lost anywhere except into the ideal universe!"

During progression in your diamond dream plans, you might be surprised with many golden chances which may settle you down wholly especially to the state where you are actually deluded yourself to be at an unexpected destination. There is presence of golden chances in the midst of the dream treasury only to appreciate your acknowledgement of each one of your wild flowers bloom. Take those golden chances to reach out your diamond destiny for a dazzling life ever.

Getting stuck in the unexpected destination, some could not recognize that they are really lost into nowhere. It is as easy as getting lost and as tough as finding yourself back. To know where you really want to settle down is to continue climbing up the higher peaks one after an other smaller ones. Consistency is not at all being perfect or trying to be perfect: rather, it is an act that protects your dream empire in reality, no matter what the outer world tries to destruct it!

By climbing up to the next higher peaks of mountains, you will be known that you are expanding a lot from within; also that you are just a speck to the eyes of universe. Importantly, you will be guided with light of nature to follow the path leading to a dazzling supreme knowledge.

Between the heights of successes you do climb up, never get deluded and lost into the materialistic world. If you do so, you will be found with your fading dream and plans that will eventually make you dwell in a state where you do not belong as you really deserve more than it. For reaching every height of the peaks that you climb up one after an other, you will be bearing all the struggles and becoming a stronger one than the prior version of yours.

Never let your dream fade just for any reason, become stronger than your previous version to know yourself and your worth.

It's absolutely not easy to be in a state of life where you don't belong: like you need to dwell in a Universe where people are not basically your type, where nature is exactly to the opposite of your favors, where you can not find a way for your future universe and the present state put you to confront many disturbances and troubles. But as we know, we can possess all the power and freedom from within to choose our dreams and actions despite all the hardships to cross the ocean and to be reached out our destination.

After reaching to the highest peak, you will know that nothing but everything in your past had happened for a good reason, reason which defines that you really belong to the state where you finally reached out: A fully grown up tree is never the same tiny sprout like in its past, but a tiny part of it is still in the tree like a tiny one. The shoots never stop to grow for moments to confront changes within itself.

"Know your worth for not falling into the state of destiny in which you will be stuck with a reason and be lost between the places and people in there."

Some are worthless to the eyes of everything, some are the worthiest to the eyes of anything and some are worthier to the eyes of nothing in this world. You could be as chaos as uncountable stars but you are the dazzling form all together anyways; you could be as dark as silent ocean but you are the deepest form to own invaluable pearls; you could be as heavy as a mighty mountain but you are the strongest form to be not just easily moved; you could be as light as a feather but you are the reason for your dream to take flights; so, you could be as powerful as a leader, but you should be as strong as a laborer to live your life as a worthwhile one.

The measures of worth for anything in the world is just created and accepted only by humans in accordance with comparisons of other things' nature and capabilities for the world; yet, the worth for ourselves, the humans can be measured beyond our potentiality in the cosmic universe as we are blessed prodigiously with a faculty to acknowledge a lot of things in life. It simply means that every soul in the world is worthy enough to be measured beyond 'everything and nothing' in the eyes of universe and we are here, on this land with a faculty to live life to the fullest. Yet, in the physical world where you dwell with your soul and body together, worth of you should be decided under the concept of what you can do in this life rather than what you got in this life.

"You are worthy to the eyes of world as you born; you are worthy to the eyes of universe when you reborn from within."

When you form yourself as a plane to make your dreams take its flights in sky, you should allow yourself to move first and fly after then. To take flights heading towards your dreams to be in reality, be the captain of the plane to lead yourself as your wish and never ever allow anyone to take in charge of you, who may change anything during your flight. It is important because, those changes would be the responses to their thoughts and actions and definitely not yours. Furthermore, the results you get from the universe for the changes in actions made by any other soul to your present universe can cause you more troubles in deserving even your own plane.

As a captain to lead towards your destinations, apart from your own decrees, listen only to the voice of the pilot, who is also you but the strong reflection of your past forms all together. Those voices and words will make yourself stronger by recognizing and accepting your own mistakes, potentials, attributes, and other faculties in you to make sure in taking the correct directions with both the great spirits together to land on the expected destinations. The roots are leading itself with a power to its shoots for making itself a stronger tree out in reality, you should acknowledge your power from within for making yourself a stronger form in your reality.

"Be the best captain who listens to pilot's words while yourself being the best pilot who always being responsible to stabilize the plane."

To fly, we should never forget our destination, also while heading towards the destination, we should never forget to feel the Zephyr between the heights we fly.

This life is a both progressive and with an ending time: not for becoming a perfect soul in the end but to never forget that we are totally perfect of being imperfect to live life to the fullest. Even though you get your mind's realm in your reality as a real figure in the physical realm, after that too, you should look after your real form in this world to make its presence for ever or else the formed figure will fade and go back as a dream again to your mind's realm eventually. The success at the end of the holy battle is not the end, that is the moment when your real battle starts and in need of ruling of something referred as consistency, the ruling battle which never ends until you wish or you are able to rule your own kingdom.

The supreme knowledge of life within yourself does not just bring to light your present parts with presence of the extreme expertise of the knowledge; rather, it makes your footprints glow in your nearest pasts and make your visions dazzle in your imminent futures too. It does not show you the right paths; rather, it makes you not to be idled but to walk in a better way on some wrong paths too. Everything that is created on this land can never be formed and appreciated without a part of this nature as a basic spirit to the resources to pool itself. So, we are not fully perfect as we are within a limit only up to our supreme knowledge in this world while the universe is playing its vital role in our journey, yet the universe is so perfect that it helps us all in a certain way to immaculate ourselves from every imperfections that we make on our own with our thoughts in mind — the only faculty need within you to lead a progressive life is to have a mastery perception in every happenings of life.

"The supreme knowledge in us that includes unique perception in life makes us understand that the light of present is so dazzling that it is invaluable and eternal in life. It always keeps the past and future locked in darkness. However, most of us are trying to run towards the darkness of irreversible past and unforeseeable future of life by not realizing that we actually make ourselves fall into nothingness. It is not good to blame or slander the universe, for only we prefer to live in the edge of life. So, acknowledge the faculty in you to live life to the fullest".

Conclusion

Like a seed of plant in land that eventually becomes a big tree out in reality, your thoughts are also seeded in your mind that at last bring your ideas in the physical realm. In the midst of this whole process, there are a lot of predicaments to be endured, the predicaments from within like being with a broken soul, trying to recognize the true self to sprout out of darkness of ignorance and endeavoring to live through the seasons in wild wood and wild flowers. Though you come a long way to reach out your destination, you must possess a will power to withhold your final form with consistency in you. For that, you must have fortitude as an attitude to improve your altitudes of your aptitude. I mean, dare to be broken for a million times to become the leader and his follower, the laborer to possess your own realm in reality.

"Spread your wings just like a plane; feel the air just like the wings of a plane and be proud with your face up that you are the pilot of your own plane!"

www.ingramcontent.com/pod-product-compliance
Lightning Source LLC
Chambersburg PA
CBHW031446150726

47990CB00007B/2638